The *Art* of

Noticing

Embracing Stress Relief and Positive Thinking through Mindful Living

Inspired by

Jay Shetty's Teachings

DAVE DRAYTON

This book is published by Therapy Seminary Publishers.

Paperback Edition: **ISBN**: 978-1-963674-17-0

First Edition: 2024

Table of Contents

FOREWARD

Do you remember truly seeing the world, not just scrolling past it? In our information frenzy, noticing is endangered, replaced by a chase for the next "like". But what if noticing isn't an old forgotten tale, but a prevalent lifestyle?

Science confirms that paying attention boosts creativity by 40%. In a multitasking world, noticing lets you focus deeply, filter distractions, and access those hidden "aha!" moments.

But the benefits go beyond work. Noticing fosters empathy and connection, battling the loneliness of our hyper-connected world. Studies link it to reduced stress and anxiety, offering a weapon against modern burnout.

The constant "hustle" thrives on our inattentiveness. By regaining the art of noticing, we break free, rediscovering the simple joys hidden in everyday moments.

This book is an invitation. Slow down, awaken your senses, and rediscover the magic waiting to be noticed. Are you ready to transform your mental health, creativity, and connection? Turn the page and let's begin.

INTRODUCTION

Have you ever stared at a blank wall, longing for an escape from the repetitious buzz of your daily routine? Do you ever wonder if the magic has faded from your world, replaced by a dull ache of "been there, done that"?

If you answered yes, you're not alone. Even the renowned life coach and former monk, Jay Shetty, once found himself yearning for something more amidst the seemingly mundane. It was through the practice of mindful observation, the very essence of what he calls "intentional living," that he rediscovered the magic hidden within the ordinary. Inspired by Shetty's transformative journey and fueled by personal experiences, this book isn't just another self-help guide promising instant happiness. It's a science-backed roadmap, informed by Shetty's teachings and his deep understanding of mindfulness, revealing the hidden magic in our everyday world.

Studies have shown that merely paying attention, a core tenet of Shetty's philosophy, has the power to:

- Light up your brain's happiness centers, igniting a spark of joy in the seemingly ordinary. Savoring such moments, as Shetty emphasizes, has proven to improve lives by boosting mental health and creativity. (Remember the last time you truly savored a sunset? Science says that wasn't just a pretty sight, it was a neurochemical boost!). A 2020 study published in Nature Neuroscience found that focused attention on positive stimuli activates the ventral striatum, a region associated with reward and pleasure.

- Sharpen your senses, transforming a routine cup of coffee into a symphony of aromas and flavors. Imagine smelling the freshly roasted beans, feeling the warmth of the mug, and appreciating the subtle notes on your tongue – a mindfulness practice disguised as your morning ritual! A 2019 study in Frontiers in Psychology demonstrated that mindfulness meditation enhances sensory perception, leading to richer experiences.

- Deepen your connections, turning fleeting interactions into meaningful moments. Imagine noticing the subtle shift in your loved one's smile, leading to a heartfelt conversation instead of another missed opportunity. Research by the Greater Good Science Center at UC Berkeley suggests that mindful attention fosters empathy and compassion, enriching relationships.

Now, I know what you're thinking: "But I already notice things! I see the traffic lights, the bills on my desk..." Ah, but herein lies the secret. The Art of Noticing, as Shetty would say, isn't about passive observation, it's about active engagement. It's about choosing to focus your attention on the often-overlooked details and everything hidden in plain sight.

This book will equip you with the tools to do just that. It's your guide to unlocking the potential of mindful observation, packed with:

- Practical exercises to awaken your senses and heighten your awareness, transforming your daily commute into a treasure hunt for sights, sounds, and smells.

- Fascinating narratives illustrate the transformative power of noticing, drawing from individuals who made groundbreaking discoveries by observing the seemingly insignificant.

- Scientific evidence that explains the "how" behind the magic, drawing on the latest research and insights from Shetty's mindfulness teachings.

The Art of Noticing isn't just a book; it's an invitation to a richer, more fulfilling life. It's a chance to break free from autopilot, rediscover the beauty in the ordinary, and tap into a wellspring of creativity and connection you never knew existed.

So, are you ready to say goodbye to the regular and hello to the extraordinary? Take a deep breath, sharpen your senses, and open the door to a world overflowing with secrets that are within your grasp. It's all waiting for you, just waiting to be noticed.

Here's an exercise that can enhance your observation skills and also help you appreciate the richness of simple visuals.

Identify 10 Items

Alright, take a peek at this mountainous landscape. It's like a scene straight out of a cozy adventure novel, right? Let's play a little game – try to find 10 things in this image that jump out at you. Take your time, absorb the details, and list them out.

How did you do? Maybe you saw:

1. The ski lift carrying people up the mountain.
2. Skiers gliding down the snowy slopes.
3. The little houses nestled among the trees.
4. A small cafe waiting to warm up the cold visitors.
5. The winding river or stream trailing through the valley.
6. A bridge crossing over the river.
7. Puffy clouds dotting the sky.
8. Snow-covered trees scattered across the landscape.
9. Smoke rising from a chimney, hinting at a warm fire inside.
10. The different genders of the skiers.

Now, let's sharpen those noticing skills. What might you have glossed over?

- The individual patterns of the ski tracks in the snow, each one telling the story of a different skier's journey.
- The delicate designs on the cafe windows, suggesting a welcoming interior.
- The sheep by the house up the mountain, evidence of life and movement.
- The poles along the ski tracks for direction and order.
- The different shapes and sizes of the ski worn by the skiers.
- The number of windows on the house down the river.

Science supports the art of noticing as a way to enhance cognitive abilities. Mindfulness practices, which involve paying full attention to the present moment, have been linked to improved cognitive flexibility, memory, and attentional skills (Zeidan et al., 2010; Moore & Malinowski, 2009). Moreover, training in visual arts can lead to significant improvements in observational skills, which are used by medical students to enhance their diagnostic abilities (Naghshineh et al., 2008).

And here's the deal – this stuff matters. Cops who get good at noticing can remember things way better. People who notice more can also come up with cooler ideas. It's all about paying attention, and it actually makes you feel better, too.

Stick with me, and by the end of the book, we'll have a bunch more of these fun exercises to do. It's like a workout for your brain, and I promise it's going to be a good time.

So, what else can you spot? Keep your eyes peeled, and let's find out.

Part I: From Blind Spots to Brilliant Insights

Our lives are a whirlwind of experiences. Images flash across screens, words pour from conversations, and the world rushes by in a blur of motion. Yet, amidst this sensory overload, how much do we truly notice? The art of noticing isn't about passive observation; it's about actively engaging with the world, cultivating curiosity, and uncovering what is hidden in plain sight. This journey of rediscovering attention promises not just fleeting moments of wonder, but a profound transformation of our lives.

Chapter 1: Wake Up, Wonder! Igniting the Spark of Curiosity

*"The important thing is not to stop questioning. Curiosity has its own reason for existing." - **Albert Einstein***

Imagine yourself as a child, eyes wide with wonder, exploring the world for the first time. Every leaf was a portal to adventure, every puddle a mirror to the unknown. But somewhere along the way, the spark of curiosity dims, replaced by the routines and responsibilities of adult life. Yet, what if I told you that reawakening that spark isn't just possible, but essential for a richer, more fulfilling life?

Curiosity isn't just about asking questions; it's a mindset, a way of engaging with the world. Dr. Barbara Fredrickson, a renowned psychologist, found that curiosity broadens our attention, allowing us to notice more details and possibilities. This expanded awareness, in turn, fosters positive emotions like joy and excitement, leading to greater creativity and problem-solving skills. Think of it like a mental muscle – the more you exercise your curiosity, the stronger and more flexible your thinking becomes.

But how do we reignite this spark in our busy, information-saturated lives? Here are a few practical steps:

1. **Ask "Why?" Like a Child**: Remember the relentless "why" questions of your childhood? Embrace them

again! Instead of accepting things at face value, challenge yourself to dig deeper. Why is that sky blue? Why does this song make me feel happy? By questioning the ordinary, you unlock hidden layers of meaning and appreciation.

2. **Embrace the Unknown**: Don't shy away from new experiences. Try a new food, explore a different neighborhood, or strike up a conversation with a stranger. Stepping outside your comfort zone exposes you to new perspectives and ignites the thrill of discovery.

3. **Play with "What If?"**: Let your imagination run wild! What if animals could talk? What if gravity suddenly stopped? Indulging in these playful questions stretches your thinking and opens doors to new ideas.

4. **Be a Noticer**: Pay attention to the small things. The way sunlight filters through leaves, the delicate pattern on a butterfly's wings, and the smile of a passerby. By focusing on these details, you cultivate a sense of wonder and appreciation for the everyday magic that surrounds us.

5. **Keep a Curiosity Journal**: Jot down questions, observations, and ideas that pique your interest. This journal becomes a source of inspiration and a reminder to maintain that curious spirit.

There will be days when the spark feels faint, but by nurturing it with these simple practices, you'll find yourself rediscovering the joy of exploration, the thrill of discovery, and the boundless opportunities that lie hidden in the world around you. So, go ahead, wake up your wonder, and embark on a life filled with the magic of noticing!

Kelvin's Experience

Hey, I'm Kelvin. Let me tell you a story about this old swing set in the park, the one that made me feel like I could fly straight into space. I was this little kid, you know, dreaming about being an astronaut. I spent countless hours there, just laughing and dreaming under those trees. But, as I got older, things changed. School, homework, and just growing up kind of took over. That swing set? It just turned into an empty frame, and my life was pretty much school, home, and staring at my phone.

My parents, they kind of faded into the background of my life. Our dinners? Nothing special, just the usual "how was your day" stuff. I was too wrapped up in my own world to notice their worried looks. Looking back now, I see all the signs I missed – those quiet moments, their forced smiles, and those long goodbyes. But back then, I was just a teen dealing with my own anxieties.

Then, everything changed when my parents decided to separate. I was just eight. My world felt like it was falling apart. I didn't know what to do, so I just buried myself in my phone. But even memes and videos couldn't fill the void I felt inside.

One day, out of the blue, a childhood friend invited me to a stargazing party. I almost didn't go, but I'm glad I did. That night, looking up at the stars, I felt something I hadn't felt in a long time – curiosity, a sense of wonder. My friend nudged me, "Remember when we wanted to be astronauts?" That hit me hard.

After that night, I started seeing the world differently. I noticed the little things – the way light fell through windows, the sound of birds in the morning, even the small smiles between strangers. It was like waking up from a long sleep.

And then, I saw my parents in a new light. I understood the pain they were going through, and I felt this wave of guilt. But instead of pulling back, I leaned in. I started asking real questions, listening to them, understanding them as people, not just my parents.

It wasn't smooth sailing. We had tough conversations, lots of tears, and some really awkward moments. But we started understanding each other better. Our family, it didn't go back to how it used to be, but it became something new and stronger.

I realized that the kid who wanted to be an astronaut was still there, just buried under everything that had happened. It took the stars, a friend's laughter, and the pain of my parents' separation to wake me up. And in waking up, I found not just them but myself too – a Kelvin who sees the world with open eyes and a heart full of wonder.

Then I discovered mindfulness. For someone who had no clue about it, it was like stepping into unknown territory. But I was ready for it. Now, I'm living life with full awareness, accepting that pain is part of it. I'm not just existing anymore; I'm living intentionally.

*"We do not see things as they are, we see them as we are conditioned to see them." - **Stephen R. Covey***

Imagine looking at a familiar painting hanging on your wall. You've probably seen it countless times, yet have you ever truly noticed the delicate brushstrokes, the hidden symbols woven into its landscape, or the emotions engraved on the figures' faces?

Our brains are wired to filter information, focusing on the familiar and essential for survival. But this filtering comes at a cost – we miss the richness and involvedness of the world around us, and often, even within ourselves.

This chapter digs into the science of attention and perception, revealing the blind spots that contribute to stress, negativity, and missed opportunities. By drawing inspiration from Jay Shetty's teachings on mindfulness and self-awareness, we'll expand our vision, both literally and figuratively.

The Invisible Gorilla Experiment

In a famous study by Dr. Daniel Simons, participants watched a video of people playing basketball. Half were instructed to count the passes made by a team in white shirts. The other half were told to watch for someone in a gorilla suit walking through the scene. Shockingly, nearly half the participants focused on counting passes and completely missed the gorilla, despite its obvious presence. This experiment highlights how our attention gets captured by specific tasks, causing us to overlook unexpected details.

Stress and the Narrow Lens

Chronic stress further narrows our focus, creating a filter for negativity. Studies by Dr. Elizabeth Phelps suggest that stress activates the amygdala, our brain's "threat detector," making us more likely to notice and dwell on negative stimuli (this is not a good factor to aid noticing especially when it becomes a regular occurrence, it negatively affects the body). This negativity bias contributes to anxiety, pessimism, and difficulty finding joy in everyday moments.

Unlocking the Potential of Seeing More

Fortunately, we can consciously expand our awareness and break free from these attentional blind spots. Mindfulness practices, as advocated by Jay Shetty, encourage us to pay attention to the present moment without judgment. By focusing on our breath, bodily sensations, and the sights and sounds around us, we activate areas of the brain associated with positive emotions and open-mindedness.

From Autopilot to Awareness

Our brains are masters of efficiency, filtering a constant barrage of information down to manageable bits. This "selective attention" serves us well, allowing us to navigate daily routines and prioritize essential tasks. Yet, like a lens focused on a single object, it blurs out the richness and complexity surrounding us.

Remember that hilarious video that had you chuckling until tears streamed down your face? Now imagine someone watching you, oblivious to the humor on your screen. That's essentially what we do to ourselves when we operate on autopilot. We miss the full spectrum of life's offerings, from the fleeting moments of joy to the subtle cues that reveal deeper truths.

The Science Behind the Seeing

This invisibility act isn't just our fault. It's rooted in the very biology of our brains. Studies by Dr. Daniel Simons, for instance, demonstrate how easily we miss obvious details when our attention is elsewhere. Think of the infamous "Invisible Gorilla" experiment, this phenomenon, known as *"inattentional blindness,"* highlights the limitations of our selective attention and the potential for missed opportunities.

But here's the good news: we're not doomed to remain oblivious observers. Neuroscience research on mindfulness, spearheaded by pioneers like Dr. Mark Williams and Dr. Jon Kabat-Zinn, reveals the transformative power of present-moment awareness. By "pausing, breathing, and being present," we break free from the autopilot mode and tap into the full tune life is playing around us.

Jay Shetty on Awareness

Jay Shetty, like a skilled conductor, guides us on a journey of mindful observation. He reminds us to "look, listen, and learn" from the world around us, highlighting the importance of curiosity, open-mindedness, and active listening. By incorporating these principles into our lives, we unlock bountiful benefits such as:

- **Stress Reduction**: Like a soothing melody washing away tension, mindfulness helps us let go of worries and anxieties, anchoring us in the present moment with a sense of calm and clarity.

- **Deeper Connections**: Imagine truly hearing the music of another's soul – that's the power of mindful listening. By paying attention to nonverbal cues and emotions beyond words, we build stronger, more meaningful relationships.

- **Enhanced Creativity**: Just as a conductor blends various instruments into one masterpiece, mindfulness opens our minds to new perspectives and connections, fostering innovation and problem-solving skills.

Practical tips to seeing beyond the obvious

Here's your conductor's baton – a collection of practices inspired by Jay Shetty's wisdom:

- **Start small**: Begin with simple exercises like mindful breathing during your commute or focusing on the taste and texture of your food.

- **Become a Curious Detective**: Cultivate a childlike curiosity, by asking questions about everything around you. Why does that crow caw? What story does that weathered brick tell?

- **Challenge Your Inner Critic**: Don't accept things at face value. Look for hidden meanings, alternative perspectives, and stories woven beneath the surface.

- **Listen Beyond Words**: Become a master of nonverbal communication. Observe body language, facial expressions, and the unspoken emotions that paint a deeper picture.

- **Embrace Technology for Good**: Utilize mindfulness apps and guided meditations as stepping stones on your journey toward present-moment awareness.

- **The "What Else?" Game**: During your day, pause and ask yourself, "What else is happening right now that I'm not noticing?" Observe sights, sounds, smells, and even your internal thoughts and emotions without judgment.

- **People Watching with Kindness**: Instead of judging passersby, practice "mindful observation." Notice their expressions, postures, and interactions with curiosity and compassion. What stories might they be carrying?

- **Nature Walks with Intention**: Instead of rushing through, slow down and truly immerse yourself in your surroundings. Feel the texture of leaves, listen to the wind rustling through branches, and appreciate the complex details of nature's beauty.

The idea isn't just in reaching the climax, but in savoring each note along the way. Here's your ticket to transform from a passive observer to an active participant in this walk of life. Welcome to a higher form of joy, connection, and creativity.

Kelvin's experience

Remember turning 30? Everyone says it's supposed to be this magical milestone, but for me, it felt like hitting a wall. Sure, I had a great job as a doctor, awesome friends, and enough money to pay the bills, but a nagging feeling wouldn't go away: something was missing.

Therapy helped clear some mental cobwebs, but I wanted something more, a tool to keep exploring myself. Then I heard meditation will do me so much good. Now, let's be honest, "meditation" made me imagine cross-legged monks chanting in some faraway temple. I mean, I'm a science-loving doc! Buddhist roots and all that... it just didn't click. But I craved something grounded, something practical, something that could benefit both my work and my life outside it.

Luckily, I found a meditation center in London that kept things real, no incense or chanting involved. These teachers were awesome, totally cool with my skeptical scientist vibe. Therapy was like the initial spark, but meditation became my go-to for constant self-reflection. Don't worry, I'm not about the whole "namaste" thing now, but the knowledge and wisdom I've gained? It's been a game-changer.

Think of it like this; meditation has become a mirror to my mind. It shows me my quirks and tendencies, but with a healthy dose of humor and self-compassion. I haven't become some enlightened guru, but I'm definitely more aware of how my thoughts and actions affect myself and others. The key? Ditching the self-judgment and criticism for some good old-fashioned self-compassion and a dash of humor. Now I can explore life with genuine curiosity, no more "fix-it" frenzy or endless self-improvement spirals.

Let's be real, starting out was rough. Sitting still, focusing on my breath, letting go? Totally against my usual "go-go-go" doctor mode. It was frustrating (and sometimes still is!). But slowly, things changed. I started handling stressful situations at work better, felt more confident in my relationships, and most importantly, truly connected with my patients on a deeper level. My newfound focus allowed me to really hear them, not just listen with half an ear.

Being present became my new way of being, both in the clinic and out. It's not always sunshine and rainbows – mindfulness forces you to see things as they are, not how you wish they were. But it also empowers you to handle any situation with both your brains and your heart.

These practices have seriously enriched my life. I take better care of myself, my patients, my family, and my friends. They've given me the courage to step outside my comfort zone, like doing those TV appearances and even writing this book! But hey, they've also allowed me to say "no" to things that drained my energy and peace of mind.

So, if you're curious, ditch the preconceived notions and explore the power of simply noticing. There's a whole world of wonder waiting to be discovered, just beyond the surface.

Chapter 3: Expanding Our Senses: Noticing Beyond Sight, Sound, and Touch

*"The world is full of magic things, patiently waiting for our senses to grow sharper." - **W.B. Yeats***

Think for a moment about the world you experience. The familiar colors that floods your vision, the sounds that fill your ears, and the textures that pleasure your fingertips. These familiar senses paint a rich picture, but they're just the first movement in a far larger picture. Welcome to the chapter that expands your sensory awareness, venturing beyond the limitations of sight, sound, and touch to know the invisible universe within and around you.

Beyond the Obvious Senses

Our five senses are incredible tools, allowing us to navigate the physical world with remarkable precision. But they're not our only tools. Studies by Dr. David Eagleman, a renowned neuroscientist, suggest that our brains process information subconsciously, often before we're consciously aware of it. This "sixth sense," sometimes referred to as intuition, allows us to pick up on little cues like changes in body language, unspoken emotions, and even energetic shifts in the environment.

Think of a time you felt a mysterious gut feeling about someone or a situation. Turns out, that hunch might have been your brain subconsciously processing silent cues you barely registered. By tuning into these whispers, we unlock a hidden dimension of understanding and can make more informed decisions.

The Science of Soft Cues

Research on biofields, conducted by pioneers like Dr. Valerie Hunt, explores the existence of an energy field surrounding our bodies. While the science is still evolving, some studies suggest this field can be influenced by emotions and even transmit information between individuals. While further research is needed, the possibility of such energy exchanges adds another layer to our sensory experience.

A Journey to Wholeness

The call for deeper awareness, for unveiling a fresher perspective through noticing, echoes across time. Socrates cautioned against the sterility of a busy life, proposing that wisdom blossoms from curiosity and that an unexamined life is simply incomplete. Lao Tzu, the sage from China, urged, "Seek within, and see, for the path to doing lies in simply being." Even Franz Kafka recognized the potential for joy in simply resting in the present experience. "No need to leave your room," he suggested. "Just sit at your table and listen. Not even listen, just wait. The world will readily reveal itself, unable to resist, unveiling its secrets at your feet."

Cultivating Stillness

Fortunately, meditation practices can act as keys to unlocking this broader view, offering a training ground for stillness and mindful attention. The practice stretches back further than recorded history – descriptions of yogic techniques appear in Hindu texts from around 2000-3000 BC, and likely predate that. Some even theorize that early humans found themselves in meditative states as they gazed in awe at flickering firelight.

Across Cultures and Within Us

This practice has woven itself into cultures worldwide, throughout the ages. Often, it takes the form of spiritual exploration, as seen in Christianity, Judaism, Islam, or shamanic rituals, a path to connecting with a deeper reality. But even without religious ties, you've likely experienced moments of intense presence – with a loved one, perhaps, or standing amidst the vastness of the sea. In these precious moments, we feel connected and attuned to our body, mind, and the world around us. Psychologist Abraham Maslow called them "**peak experiences**," and while they can occur naturally, meditation can cultivate their frequency but can't be forced.

Measuring with Awareness

The very word "**meditation**" stems from the Indo-European root "med," meaning "to measure." When we engage with something mindfully, we are observing it with gentle curiosity and equanimity, striving to see it for what it truly is, unencumbered by our mental projections. This is the essence of measuring with awareness.

Jay Shetty's Call to Awaken Our Senses

Jay Shetty, a mindfulness expert and advocate for holistic well-being, encourages us to "connect with the unseen forces" within and around us. He emphasizes the importance of "cultivating our intuition" and trusting the whispers that guide us. Through practices like meditation and mindful awareness, we can learn to perceive these mild cues and harness their wisdom.

Expanding Your Sensory Repertoire

So, how do we start tuning into this invisible universe?

Here are a few practices inspired by Jay Shetty's teachings:

1. **The Sensory Scavenger Hunt:**

   - **Sight**: Choose a familiar environment, like your living room or a park. Sit quietly and observe, truly seeing beyond the obvious. Notice details you usually miss – the patterns in the rug, the texture of a leaf, the way light dances on a wall. Close your eyes briefly and then open them, allowing your vision to refresh and discover new details.

   - **Sound**: Take a walk outside or sit in a quiet space. Focus on the soundscape around you. Can you hear the chirping of birds, the rustling of leaves, the distant hum of traffic? Close your eyes and listen intently. What new sounds emerge from the background?

- **Touch**: Hold an object you haven't touched in a while – a smooth stone, a piece of fabric, a feather. Close your eyes and focus on the sensations at your fingertips. Is it cold, rough, or soft? Can you feel its weight, texture, and energy?

- **Smell**: Light a scented candle or open a jar of spices. Close your eyes and inhale deeply, allowing the aroma to fill your senses. Can you identify different notes? Does the scent evoke any memories or emotions?

- **Taste**: Take a bite of food, savoring it slowly. Notice the different textures on your tongue, the flavors unfolding, and the sensations it creates in your mouth. Can you taste subtle nuances you usually miss?

2. **The Mindful Body Scan:**

- Lie down comfortably in a quiet space and close your eyes. Focus your attention on your toes, noticing any sensations like warmth, tingling, or pressure. Slowly move your attention up your body, part by part, observing any sensations without judgment. Do you feel any energy blockages or areas of tension? Acknowledge them and let them go.

- As you scan your body, pay attention to any emotions that arise. Are there areas of sadness, joy, or anxiety? Gently observe them without judgment, allowing them to flow through you.

- This practice can help you become more in harmony with your internal cues, including subtle energy shifts that might offer valuable insights.

3. **The Energy Exchange Experiment:**

- Sit facing a partner and close your eyes. Spend a few minutes quieting your mind and connecting with your inner energy. Imagine a warm, golden light emanating from your heart.

- When you feel ready, silently open your eyes and gaze into your partner's eyes with kindness and curiosity. Imagine sending your warm light to them, and receiving their energy in return.

- After a few minutes, share your experiences. Did you feel any shifts in energy? Did you sense any emotions or information from your partner? Remember, this is a playful practice, not a competition.

4. **Nature's Symphony:**

- Spend time in nature, immersing yourself in the sights, sounds, and smells. Walk barefoot on the earth, feeling the connection to the ground. Listen to the wind rustling through the leaves, the birdsong, the chatting brook, and the sweet smell of the summer breeze. Close your eyes and sense the energy of the trees, the sun, the earth beneath you.

- Pay attention to any intuitive nudges you receive. Does a certain tree call to you? Does a particular path feel more inviting? Trust your inner guidance and see where it leads you.

5. **The Silent Conversation:**

- Choose a quiet moment when you're alone, free from distractions. Sit comfortably and close your eyes. Focus on your breath, calming your mind.

- Ask a question to your intuition, to your inner wisdom, or to the universe. It could be about a decision you're facing, a challenge you're overcoming, or simply a desire for guidance.

- Be patient and listen. The answer might not come in a clear voice or vision. It could be a subtle feeling, a thought that pops into your head, or a dream you have later.

- Trust the process. The more you practice this silent conversation, the more attuned you'll become to the subtle whispers of your intuition.

Experiment, be playful, and trust your intuition. As you practice these exercises regularly, you'll gradually expand your sensory awareness and unlock the hidden dimensions of your experience. The more attuned you become to the invisible universe within and around you, the richer and more fulfilling your life will become.

Sophia's experience

Let me tell you about my dear friend Sophia who is now a mindfulness master, although it took her 7 years to get this good! Her story reveals the benefits of paying attention to not just the sights, sounds, and smells around us but about the world beyond.

Back in '92, when "Smells Like Teen Spirit" was rocking the airwaves, Sophia was dealing with stress at her radio producer job although her true passion was tech, and promised herself to do what she truly loves someday. Her eczema became more pronounced, revealing the troubles she was experiencing inside.

Seeking solace, she grabbed a meditation book at the airport, hoping it might be her Xanax in disguise. And guess what? Under a fig tree in Corsica, the magic began.

Meditation opened a portal to calm but soon became more than just stress relief. A weekend retreat ignited a deeper transformation. "It felt like stepping outside my head," Sophia explains, "like the world was in technicolor." No more being trapped in thought loops, the vastness of existence unfolded before her.

But wait, wasn't meditation some religious mumbo jumbo? Sophia, initially wary, researched deeper. The Buddhist wisdom resonated with her newfound awareness. It wasn't about becoming someone different but embracing who she was, flaws and all. And boy, did that unleash change!

Before meditation, Sophia was like a speeding bullet, missing 99% of her life. Food? Tasteless. Walks? Blurry. Touch? Meaningless. But her practice taught her to let go of thought patterns and be present. Now, she paid attention to every detail, even the patterns on trees. She no longer dwelt on the past nor fret about the future, just pure, joyful aliveness.

And when pressure mounts? She doesn't explode like a firecracker anymore, now she knows only she can control how she reacts. The stress she once experienced became a thing of the past and to her amazement, her eczema vanished!

Sophia learnt to be consistent. As the days passed, her mindfulness muscle strengthened. She spent not less than 20-minute daily every morning meditating to set the tone for noticing throughout the day.

But Sophia's journey goes beyond the usual sights, sounds, and touch. She also learned a deeper level of awareness – a mindful communion with the world around and within her.

So, the next time you feel like you're running on autopilot, take a moment. Breathe. Notice. You might just discover a whole new world unfolding, right beneath your feet.

Part II: Unveiling the Extraordinary in the Everyday

Look around you. Do you see the ordinary, or do you see the extraordinary waiting to be discovered? We are about to go deeper into the art of noticing, not just with your eyes, but with your heart and mind. We'll explore the hidden language of nonverbal communication, revealing the secrets that lie beneath the surface of everyday interactions. Then, we'll venture into ways active noticing can improve the state of our health and our general well-being. Finally, we'll ignite the spark within, using the power of noticing to unleash your creative potential and transform the ordinary into the extraordinary.

Prepare to shift your perspective, challenge your assumptions, and rediscover the excellence that floods our every moment. Let's begin.

Chapter 4: Decoding the Unspoken: Noticing What Words Don't Say

"The most eloquent speech is often that which is never said."
*- **Ralph Waldo Emerson***

Words are powerful tools, shaping our thoughts, conveying emotions, and building connections. But in human interaction, words are just one instrument in a much larger universe. Often, the most profound messages resonate beyond the words we speak, hidden in the whispers of nonverbal communication. Here we are looking at the art of "decoding the unspoken," a skill that unlocks deeper understanding, strengthens relationships, empowers you to navigate the complexities of human connection, and helps build you an armor for loneliness and modern burnout like many are hawking as trophies these days.

The Power of Nonverbal Communication

Think about a time you felt misunderstood, despite using your words carefully. It's likely the message you conveyed didn't align with the nonverbal cues you unknowingly emitted – your posture, tone of voice, or facial expression contradicting your spoken words. Research by Dr. Mehrabian, a pioneer in nonverbal communication, suggests that 7% of communication is based on words, 38% on vocal cues, and

55% on facial expressions. This means that over 90% of our message is conveyed nonverbally!

So, what are these nonverbal cues, and how can we learn to "speak" and "listen" to them more effectively?

The Language of the Body

Our bodies are constantly sending messages, even when our lips are sealed. Posture, gestures, and facial expressions form a complex language that reveals emotions, intentions, and even hidden truths. A crossed arm might signal defensiveness, a wrinkled brow could indicate confusion and a genuine smile can convey warmth and trust. By becoming more aware of these cues, we can gain deeper insights into the thoughts and feelings of others, even when their words remain unspoken.

The Science of Micro expressions

Research by Dr. Paul Ekman, a renowned psychologist, revealed the existence of micro expressions, fleeting facial expressions that last less than a second but can reveal hidden emotions. While consciously masking emotions is possible, these microexpressions often betray our true feelings, offering a glimpse into the subconscious mind. Learning to recognize these fleeting expressions can equip you to decode unspoken messages and navigate even the most challenging conversations.

The Melody of the Voice

Our voices hold hidden messages beyond the words themselves. The tone, pitch, and volume all convey emotions and intentions. A monotone voice might signal boredom or disinterest, while a rising pitch can indicate excitement or confusion. By paying attention to the melody of someone's voice, you can gain valuable insights into their emotional state and the true meaning behind their words.

The Power of Silence

Silence, often seen as an absence of communication, can be a powerful tool in its own right. A comfortable silence can signify mutual understanding and trust, while an awkward silence might indicate tension or unspoken conflict. Even the length of pauses between words can convey meaning, with longer pauses suggesting deeper thought or hesitation. Learning to listen to and interpret silence allows you to engage in meaningful conversations.

Jay Shetty on Active Listening

Jay Shetty emphasizes the importance of "active listening", where we go beyond simply hearing words and focus on understanding the full message, including the nonverbal cues. He encourages us to "listen with our eyes, our hearts, and our whole being." By practicing active listening, we can build stronger relationships, resolve conflicts more effectively, and foster deeper connections with others.

Jay Shetty encourages us to rise above the limitations of words and truly "connect at a soul level" through the unspoken language of nonverbal communication. He reminds us that "words can lie, but our body language never does," urging us to become keen observers of the world around us.

One of Shetty's powerful teachings emphasizes the "power of presence" in communication. He encourages us to be fully present in our interactions, "quieting the mind and tuning into the energy" that flows between us. By being present, we can tap into nonverbal cues to foster deeper connections and build trust.

Shetty recounts a story of misinterpreting a friend's crossed arms as negativity, only to later discover they were simply cold. This experience out of countless more underscores the crucial role of context and cultural awareness in accurately interpreting nonverbal cues.

Unlocking the Secrets of Nonverbal Communication

So, how do we nurture this skill of decoding the unspoken? Here are a few practices inspired by Jay Shetty's teachings:

- **Mirror the Microexpressions**:

  Mirror the microexpressions of others to build rapport and encourage them to feel safe and understood.

- **Practice Active Listening**: Focus on the speaker's entire message, paying attention to their nonverbal cues as much as their words. Ask clarifying questions and avoid interrupting to ensure you understand the full message.

- **Become a Student of Body Language**: Learn about common nonverbal cues and their potential meanings. Remember, context is crucial, and a single cue should not be interpreted in isolation.

- **Mindful Observation:** Practice observing others with curiosity and non-judgment. Notice their posture, facial expressions, gestures, and voice patterns without labeling or interpreting them prematurely.

- **Embrace Silence**: Don't feel pressured to fill every pause with words. Allow comfortable silences to develop and learn to listen to their messages.

A deeper dive into some advanced nonverbal communication techniques

Beyond the basic understanding of facial expressions and body language lies a fascinating world of advanced nonverbal communication techniques. These tools, while requiring dedication and practice, can significantly enhance your ability to decode the unspoken messages that flow around you. Let's delve into three key concepts and explore some additional possibilities for further research:

1. A Deeper Dive into Micro Expressions

Imagine catching a glimpse of genuine disgust masked by a polite smile, or witnessing a flicker of fear before it's consciously bottled up. These fleeting facial expressions, lasting mere milliseconds, are known as micro-expressions. While mastering the art of recognizing them requires extensive training, even basic awareness can equip you to pick up on hidden emotions and intentions.

Research by Dr. Paul Ekman, a pioneer in nonverbal communication, has identified seven universal microexpressions: *happiness, sadness, anger, fear, surprise, disgust, and contempt.* However, interpreting them accurately requires considering context, cultural norms, and individual differences. A wrinkled brow might indicate concentration in one situation but annoyance in another. Dr. Ekman's Facial Action Coding System (FACS) or specialized training programs throw more light on non-verbal communication.

2. Proxemics: The Language of Personal Space

Imagine feeling uncomfortable when someone stands too close, or misinterpreting a colleague's open posture as flirtatious. Proxemics, the study of how we use personal space, plays a crucial role in nonverbal communication. Understanding cultural norms surrounding personal space is essential to avoid misinterpretations.

For instance, in North American cultures, a larger personal space is typically preferred, while in some Asian cultures, standing closer might be considered normal. Recognizing these differences can prevent awkward situations and foster smoother interactions.

Beyond cultural awareness, proxemics can also reveal emotional states and intentions. An individual who leans in closely might be displaying interest or confidence, while someone maintaining a larger distance could indicate discomfort or disinterest. By observing how individuals use personal space in different contexts, you can gain valuable insights into their emotions and intentions.

3. Kinesics: The Study of Body Movement

From twitching fingers to crossed arms, our bodies speak volumes through movement. Kinesics, the study of body language, explores how gestures, posture, and even unintended shifts in weight distribution convey information. While some gestures might have universal meanings (e.g., a thumbs-up for approval), interpreting kinesics effectively requires considering context and cultural norms.

For example, a hand on the hip might indicate confidence in one culture, while in another, it could be perceived as aggression. Additionally, individual differences play a role. Someone who naturally folds their arms might not be closed off, but simply comfortable in that posture.

By observing and interpreting body language in conjunction with other nonverbal cues and the context of the interaction, you can gain valuable insights into a person's emotions, intentions, and personality traits.

Exploring Further Frontiers

The journey into advanced nonverbal communication doesn't end here. Here are some additional avenues for exploration:

- **Vocal Cues**: Beyond words, listen to the nuances of voice. Pitch, tone, and even silence can convey emotions and intentions. For instance, a monotone voice might indicate boredom, while a hesitant tone could suggest uncertainty.

- **Eye Contact**: While prolonged eye contact can be uncomfortable in some cultures, understanding its role in different contexts is crucial. Direct eye contact can convey confidence and interest, while averted gaze might indicate nervousness or discomfort.

- **Chronemics**: How individuals use time can also be revealing. Punctuality, willingness to wait, and even speaking pace can convey cultural norms, personality traits, and even respect levels.

- **Haptics**: Touch, though often underutilized in professional settings, can be a powerful nonverbal cue. Understanding cultural norms surrounding touch and interpreting its use appropriately is crucial.

By integrating mindful listening and a willingness to learn, you can unlock the hidden messages that flow around you, enriching your life and fostering deeper connections with the world.

Additional Tips to note:

- Practice makes perfect: Observe nonverbal cues in everyday interactions and discuss your observations with trusted friends or colleagues.

- Seek feedback: Ask friends or colleagues to provide honest feedback on your own nonverbal communication, helping you identify areas for improvement.

- Embrace cultural sensitivity: Remember, there's no one-size-fits-all approach to nonverbal communication. Always consider cultural norms and individual differences.

- Combine with mindful listening: Nonverbal cues offer valuable insights, but true understanding comes from combining them with active and mindful listening.

Noticing the unspoken fosters **deeper connections**. Words can be misleading, but body language rarely lies. By reading these cues – a warm smile, a reassuring touch, or even a shared silence – you can connect with others on a deeper level, building trust, empathy, and a sense of belonging. This social connection is vital for our well-being, reducing stress and boosting our happiness. Imagine a tense conversation with a loved one. By noticing the discomfort in their furrowed brow or averted gaze, you can shift your approach, de-escalate the situation, and mend the connection, fostering a healthier and happier relationship.

Also, noticing the unspoken can **protect us from burnout**. In our fast-paced world, demands pile up, pushing us towards exhaustion. But often, the first signs of burnout appear not in words, but in subtle shifts. A clenched jaw, a habitual frown, or constantly checking your phone – these can be early warning signs of stress and impending burnout. By becoming attuned to these cues, you can recognize the need to slow down, prioritize self-care, and prevent burnout before it takes hold. Imagine feeling overwhelmed at work. Noticing your tense posture and shallow breathing can prompt you to take a mindful break, practice deep breathing exercises, and regain your composure, safeguarding your mental and physical health.

Furthermore, noticing the unspoken can enhance your communication skills. Words are powerful, but they're only half the story. By combining your words with consistent nonverbal cues, you can express yourself more authentically and effectively. Imagine giving a presentation. Understanding the impact of your posture, eye contact, and gestures allows you to connect with your audience, project confidence, and deliver your message with greater clarity and impact. This improved communication empowers you in various aspects of life, from thriving in professional settings to navigating personal relationships effectively.

Noticing the unspoken can cultivate empathy and understanding. When we pay attention to the world around us, not just the words uttered, we begin to see things from other perspectives. By understanding the emotions and intentions behind the unspoken, we can practice empathy, build bridges with others, and foster a more harmonious and compassionate world. Imagine encountering someone who seems upset. Instead of jumping to conclusions based on their limited words, noticing their tearful eyes and trembling hands allows you to offer genuine support and understanding, creating a positive impact on their well-being.

Lastly, noticing the "words not spoken" isn't just about reading minds. It's about enriching your understanding of the world around you, connecting with others on a deeper level, and ultimately cultivating a healthier, happier, and more resilient life. So, step into the bustling marketplace of everyday interactions, but remember to listen not just to the shouts, but also to the whispers of the unspoken language. You might be surprised at the wisdom and connection you discover.

Sophia's Experience

Sophia finally transitioned to tech, she landed running and in no time became a tech whiz with a mind wired for efficiency. She was a master of deciphering digital languages but nonverbal communication remained a frustrating mystery. Emails and texts were her comfort zone, devoid of the messy emotions and hidden subtext that hid beneath spoken words.

One day, while attending a workshop, Sophia stumbled upon the concept of "decoding the unsaid." It was like a revelation. Suddenly, the world around her became a pile of nonverbal cues - a wrinkled brow, a hesitant smile, a lingering gaze - each holding a story waiting to be exposed.

Intrigued, Sophai embarked on a mindful quest to observe and interpret these silent languages. She started with her colleagues, noticing their posture during presentations, the way their eyes moved when they disagreed, and the warmth in their smiles when they were genuinely happy. Slowly, the unsaid words began to translate into meaningful conversations, fostering deeper connections and a deeper understanding of her team.

Beyond the workplace, Sophia's newfound awareness blossomed in her personal life. She learned to read the unspoken language of her loved ones - the hidden worry in her mother's forced laughter, the unspoken support in her partner's reassuring touch, and the unspoken joy in her child's shy giggle. These cues, once hidden, became bridges of empathy, strengthening the bonds she cherished.

But the journey wasn't without its challenges. Misinterpretations happened, and awkward silences followed. Yet, Sophia persevered, learning from each fumble, realizing that "decoding the unsaid" wasn't about perfection, but about a willingness to listen beyond words.

As Sophis's practice deepened, she discovered the transformative power of her newfound skill. She became a better communicator, expressing her own emotions more authentically, and a more compassionate listener, truly hearing what people were saying, not just with their words, but with their entire being.

Sophia's story is a reminder that the art of noticing extends beyond the obvious. By tuning into the unspoken language that surrounds us, we unlock a deeper understanding of ourselves and the world, fostering meaningful connections and enriching our lives in ways we never thought.

Chapter 5: The Art of noticing for optimal health, beauty, and general wellbeing

"Burnout isn't a status symbol; it's a slow fade-out." -
Emily Nagoski, Amelia Nagoski

This practice of truly **noticing** the beauty and wonder surrounding us holds the key to unlocking a life overflowing with good health, beauty, relief of stress, positive thinking and overall well-being. In this chapter, get ready to be transformed by cultivating the art of noticing in your everyday life.

Fueling Wellbeing through Awareness

Today, we often find ourselves on autopilot, rushing from one task to another without truly being present at the moment. This constant state of mental busyness can lead to chronic stress, anxiety, and disconnect from our bodies and the world around us. Jay Shetty emphasizes the importance of "quieting the mind and tuning into the present moment" as the foundation for true well-being. By practicing the art of noticing, we step off autopilot and reconnect with our senses, fostering a sense of calm, clarity, and appreciation.

Studies by Dr. Herbert Benson, a pioneer in mindfulness research, have shown that mindful practices like focused attention on the present moment can trigger the relaxation response, lowering stress hormones and promoting physical and mental well-being. Imagine **savoring** the taste and texture of your food instead of mindlessly scrolling through your phone while eating. This simple act of noticing can enhance your digestion, improve your relationship with food, and cultivate a sense of gratitude for nourishment.

Let's talk about the art of noticing for good health, beauty, and general wellbeing;

Noticing to reveal the Beauty from within

The world around us is jam-packed with beauty, waiting to be discovered by the attentive eye. A single dewdrop glittering on a spider web, the sophisticated patterns on a ladybug, the laughter of a child at play – these seemingly ordinary moments hold extraordinary beauty when we take the time to truly notice them. As Jay Shetty reminds us, "Beauty is everywhere if we just open our eyes to see it."

Research conducted by Dr. Ulrich Lohmar, a renowned environmental psychologist, suggests that exposure to nature can have a profound impact on mental and emotional well-being. Immersing ourselves in natural beauty, whether it's a walk in the park or simply observing a potted plant on our windowsill, can reduce stress, improve mood, and even boost our creativity. Imagine pausing to admire the vibrant colors of the sunset instead of rushing to your next appointment. This simple act of noticing can leave you feeling more energized, inspired, and connected to the world around you.

Noticing Your Way to Calmness and relief from Stress

Chronic stress is a major contributor to various health problems, both physical and mental. But what if the antidote lies in the simple act of noticing? By tuning into our senses, we can activate the parasympathetic nervous system, promoting relaxation and stress relief.

Studies by Dr. Jon Kabat-Zinn, a leading figure in mindfulness research, have demonstrated the effectiveness of mindfulness-based stress reduction (MBSR) programs in reducing anxiety, depression, and chronic pain. By focusing on the sensations in our bodies, we can shift our attention away from worries and anxieties, promoting a sense of calm and grounding. Imagine focusing on the rhythmic sound of your breath as you walk, instead of dwelling on your to-do list. This simple act of noticing can help you release tension, quiet your mind, and find moments of peace amidst the daily grind.

Noticing your way to thinking positively through gratitude

Our thoughts and perspectives have a profound impact on our overall well-being. By cultivating an attitude of gratitude and appreciation for the good things in our lives, we can shift our focus from negativity to positivity, encouraging a sense of happiness and contentment. Jay Shetty encourages us to "practice daily gratitude, acknowledging the little things that make life beautiful."

Research by Dr. Robert Emmons, a renowned gratitude researcher, has shown that practicing gratitude can lead to increased happiness, reduced stress, and improved sleep quality. By taking time to notice and appreciate the blessings in our lives, big or small, we cultivate a positive mindset that enhances our overall well-being. Imagine pausing before each meal to acknowledge the farmers, chefs, and everyone involved in bringing the food to your plate. This simple act of noticing can cultivate gratitude, foster positive emotions, and enhance your enjoyment of the meal.

Recognizing the Early Signs

Burnout, characterized by emotional exhaustion, cynicism, and reduced personal efficiency, can significantly impact our physical and mental health. However, the art of noticing can help us identify the early signs before they escalate. By observing our body language, energy levels, and emotional responses to daily stressors, we can adjust our routines and prioritize self-care practices. Imagine noticing that you're clenching your jaw and feeling irritable at work. This act of noticing prompts you to take a deep breath, stretch your muscles, and perhaps delegate some tasks, preventing burnout and safeguarding your well-being.

Burnout becoming a global menace

Studies by Dr. Christina Maslach, a leading researcher on burnout, reveal its alarming prevalence, affecting individuals across professions and demographics. This widespread issue has significant consequences, impacting not only individual well-being but also productivity, relationships, and overall quality of life.

Early Signs of Burnout

Burnout creeps in quietly, often masquerading as everyday fatigue or stress. But beneath the surface, silent but evident changes are taking place inside that go unnoticed. Here's where the art of noticing becomes your shield against burnout:

- **Physical Cues:** Notice changes in your body – persistent headaches, disrupted sleep, weakened immune system, or unexplained aches and pains. These are often the first hints of burnout's presence.

- **Emotional Shifts:** Pay attention to your emotional setting. Increased irritability, cynicism, detachment, or a sense of emotional numbness can signal burnout's sinister grip.

- **Mental Fog:** Difficulty concentrating, forgetfulness, or a decline in creativity can be early signs of burnout's impact on your cognitive function.

- **Behavioral Changes:** Do you isolate yourself from social interactions? Do you neglect hobbies you once enjoyed? Or do you engage in unhealthy coping mechanisms like substance abuse? All there can be red flags for burnout.

Jay Shetty's Call to Burnout Awareness

Jay Shetty emphasizes the importance of "recognizing the warning signs" of burnout before it takes hold. He encourages us to "listen to the whispers of our bodies and minds" and promote a practice of "mindful awareness" to recognize the quiet shifts that signal impending burnout. His teaching buttresses the power of noticing and we will talk more about it below.

Active Strategies to Ignite the Power Noticing

Noticing isn't passive observation; it's active engagement with your inner and outer world. Here are some strategies inspired by Jay Shetty's teachings to hone your noticing skills:

- **Mindful Body Scans:** Regularly take time to scan your body, noticing any physical sensations, tightness, or discomfort. This practice can help you identify early signs of stress and burnout before they escalate.

- **Journaling with Intention:** Dedicate time each day to journaling, reflecting on your emotions, thoughts, and experiences. This introspective practice can help you identify patterns and recognize subtle shifts that might indicate burnout.

- **Gratitude Practices:** Cultivating gratitude can shift your perspective and build resilience against stress. Regularly expressing gratitude for the good things in your life can counter the negativity that often fuels burnout.

- **Nature Connection:** Spend time in nature, immersing yourself in the sights, sounds, and smells of the natural world. Studies show that nature exposure can reduce stress, improve mood, and boost well-being, offering a powerful antidote to burnout.

Building Resilience

Noticing is just the first step. Building resilience against burnout requires proactive measures:

- **Set Boundaries:** Learn to say no and establish healthy boundaries between work and personal life. Prioritize rest, relaxation, and activities that bring you joy.

- **Connect with Others:** Social support is crucial. Cultivate meaningful connections with friends, family, and loved ones. Sharing your struggles and seeking support can provide strength and encouragement.

- **Seek Professional Help:** If you're struggling to manage burnout on your own, don't hesitate to seek professional help. Therapists and counselors can provide valuable guidance and support in developing coping mechanisms and building resilience.

BONUS ON SUFFERING...

The Four Honorable Truths to note on suffering according to the Buddha

Life can be like a wild rollercoaster, you're strapped in, dragged up and down, and made to bear every twist and turn. Sometimes the wind whips through your hair, excitement bubbling in your chest. Other times, you're plunged into darkness, fear gripping your throat. This is the human experience...

Below are four honorable truths to note about suffering by Buddha.

Truth #1: The Ride's Bumpy

We all know the sting of suffering – birth, sickness, aging, death, and the emotional turmoil that comes with them. It's unavoidable, like the first drop on a rollercoaster ride. But unlike passive passengers, we often react poorly.

Truth #2: Craving is the Second Drop

Imagine clinging to the handrails for dear life, resisting the dips and dives. That's craving – desperately grasping for pleasure and pushing away pain. It's the second drop on the ride, amplifying the fear and discomfort. We crave things beyond our control – eternal youth, perfect relationships, and a life free of hardship. This resistance creates more suffering than the initial bumps themselves.

Truth #3: There's an Exit (But Not the One You Think)

The good news? We're not stuck forever. The third truth offers a way out, not by escaping the ride, but by changing how we experience it.

Truth #4: The Eightfold Path - Your Ticket to a Smoother Ride

Think of the eightfold path as a guide to navigating the rollercoaster. It's not about wishing the ride away, but about developing skills to handle the twists and turns with grace. It's about right understanding (accepting impermanence), right thought (letting go of resistance), right action (living ethically), right mindfulness (being present), and more.

Instead of white-knuckling it, you learn to lean into the turns, appreciating the thrill and the view. You see the interconnectedness of everyone on the ride, offering compassion and support. The bumps are still there, but the fear lessens, replaced by a sense of flow and acceptance.

This isn't about blind optimism, but about cultivating wisdom and resilience. It's about transforming your experience, not the ride itself. So, take a deep breath, loosen your grip, and embrace the journey. You might just find yourself enjoying the ride, arrows and all.

The place of Happy Hormones in protecting us from Stress, Burnout, and Negative thoughts

The four "happy hormones" - dopamine, serotonin, endorphins, and oxytocin - play a powerful role in shaping our mood, resilience, and ability to cope with challenges. Research reveals the fascinating mechanisms by which these powerful molecules combat stress and burnout, and foster positive thinking, resilience, and general well-being.

1.   Dopamine: The Reward System Warrior

Imagine the satisfaction of finally finishing a project or the pure joy of laughter shared with friends. Dopamine, the reward hormone, thrives on such moments. Research suggests it not only fuels pleasure but also motivates us to seek out positive experiences. A 2019 study published in Nature Neuroscience found that dopamine signaling plays a crucial role in optimistic decision-making, guiding us toward choices with anticipated rewards. This, in turn, can help combat negativity and foster a more positive outlook.

2.   Serotonin: The Mood Regulator on Duty

Serotonin's influence goes beyond just feeling good. Studies have linked adequate serotonin levels to reduced stress reactivity, improved emotional resilience, and better sleep quality. A 2018 study in JAMA Psychiatry found that a serotonin-regulating medication effectively reduced stress-related symptoms in individuals with anxiety disorders. Moreover, a 2017 review in Frontiers in Behavioral Neuroscience highlighted the connection between serotonin and cognitive flexibility, essential for adapting to challenges and finding solutions.

3.   Endorphins: The Natural Pain Tamers

Ever felt the adrenaline rush after a great workout? That's the endorphins kicking in. These natural painkillers not only numb physical discomfort but also elevate mood and reduce stress perception. Research published in Psychoneuroendocrinology in 2017 demonstrated that regular exercise significantly increased endorphin levels, leading to decreased stress and improved emotional well-being. Interestingly, a 2020 study in Nature Human Behaviour found that even laughter triggers endorphin release, contributing to stress reduction and increased social bonding.

4.   Oxytocin: The Social Connection Catalyst

Oxytocin, often dubbed the "love hormone," strengthens our social bonds. It's released during physical touch, childbirth, and breastfeeding, fostering feelings of trust, empathy, and attachment. Research published in Nature Neuroscience in 2019 revealed that oxytocin administration promotes positive social interactions and reduces stress reactivity, offering a buffer against burnout. Additionally, a 2015 study in

Proceedings of the National Academy of Sciences found that oxytocin enhances our ability to perceive positive emotions in others, further contributing to a more optimistic outlook.

It's crucial to remember that these happy hormones don't operate in isolation. They work together, creating a symphony of well-being. For instance, exercise not only boosts endorphins but also promotes serotonin production, while the social connection can trigger both oxytocin and dopamine release.

Harnessing the Power of happy hormones for better living

The good news is that we can actively influence our happy hormone levels through daily choices:

- **Exercise regularly:** Get your endorphins pumping with the physical activity you enjoy.

- **Connect with loved ones:** Foster social bonds and experience the magic of oxytocin. Don't forget to call up these memories shared often to savor these beautiful moments again and again; this will foster these happy hormones to dwell longer in you.

- **Practice gratitude:** Expressing thankfulness elevates both dopamine and serotonin.

- **Spend time in nature:** Sunlight exposure promotes serotonin production.

- **Eat a balanced diet:** Certain foods, like fruits and vegetables, support healthy hormone levels.

- **Prioritize sleep:** Adequate rest is crucial for optimal hormone production.

So, what's the takeaway? Embrace the power of these happy hormones. Conduct your own well-being by incorporating activities that boost dopamine, serotonin, endorphins, and oxytocin into your life. Remember, small changes can lead to big results. Step outside for sunshine, laugh with loved ones, move your body, connect with others, and nourish your body with healthy foods. As you do, you'll find yourself humming a happier tune, resilient against stress, and radiating positive thinking.

Kelvin's Experience

Once, I was called – "CEO with many hats". When I took the job of an administrator for a struggling baking company, stress became my constant companion. Between studing for my PLAB exam and single parenting, I desperately needed a way to breathe. Thankfully, my company offered a wellness perk: Mindfulness-Based Cognitive Therapy.

At first, meditation seemed like just another way to unwind. But soon, it transformed into a powerful tool. "Thoughts aren't facts," became my mantra, reminding me to step back from automatic negativity. Instead of getting swept away by anger or resentment, I learned to acknowledge them without judgment. The result? A calmer, more positive workplace presence, even under pressure.

But the benefits went beyond work. As I grappled with the hurt of my past relationship, mindfulness offered a healing touch. After years of therapy, it helped me mend fences with my ex, fostering a kinder, and more amicable connection. This newfound inner peace allowed me to offer more support to those around me.

As someone who lost my parents young, the idea of self-parenting resonated deeply with me. When feelings of abandonment arose, a quick meditation session became my go-to remedy. This practice offered a sense of self-reliance, replacing the yearning for external validation.

I believe many underestimate the importance of mental well-being, especially in our fast-paced world. While gyms and healthy eating are priorities, emotional fitness often gets neglected. We live in a demanding environment, "Mindfulness allows us to savor the good stuff, like a friendly cashier or a beautiful sunset. It's about choosing to notice the joy in everyday moments."

So, next time you feel overwhelmed, take a mindful pause. Remember, just like me, you have the power to cultivate inner peace and navigate life's challenges with grace and resilience.

"Creativity is intelligence having fun." - **Albert Einstein**

Do you ever feel the spark of inspiration flicker within you, only to have it extinguished by the daily routine? The truth is, creativity isn't a magical gift bestowed upon a selected few; it's a hidden potential within each of us, waiting to be ignited. And the key to unlocking this potential lies in the simple act of **noticing**. Inspired by the wisdom of Jay Shetty, who emphasizes the importance of "quieting the mind and tuning into the present moment," this chapter explores ways to cultivate the art of noticing to unleash a powerful wellspring of creativity and combat the burnout that often stifles it.

The Neuroscience of Noticing for Creativity

Recent research in **neuroplasticity**, the brain's ability to change and adapt, provides exciting insights into the transformative power of noticing. Studies suggest that focusing our attention on specific aspects of the world can strengthen neural pathways associated with creativity. This means that by practicing the art of noticing, we can rewire our brains to be more creative and innovative.

Furthermore, research on **mirror neurons**, brain cells that fire both when we perform an action and when we observe someone else doing it, suggests that observing creative acts can stimulate our creative potential. So, surrounding yourself with creative individuals and actively engaging with their work can further enhance your creative journey.

Disconnection, a crisis to Creativity

In a world dominated by screens and schedules, our ability to truly **notice** has become increasingly diminished. We rush through our days, bombarded with information but rarely taking the time to absorb, reflect, and engage with the world around us. This constant state of mental busyness fuels stress, anxiety, and burnout, leaving little room for the spark of creativity to ignite.

Research by Dr. Mihaly Csikszentmihalyi, a renowned psychologist, highlights the importance of **flow** states, characterized by complete immersion and absorption in an activity. These states, often associated with creativity, are difficult to achieve when our minds are cluttered and our attention is constantly fragmented. By practicing the art of noticing, we can quiet the mental chatter, enter a state of mindful presence, and create fertile ground for creative expression.

Noticing as a Catalyst for Inspiration

Pause for a moment and look around you. What do you see? Creativity begins with curiosity and the desire to explore the world around us.

Studies by Dr. Scott Barry Kaufman, a leading creativity researcher, suggest that **divergent thinking**, the ability to generate multiple unique ideas, is a cornerstone of creativity. By noticing the unexpected, the overlooked, and the seemingly insignificant details, we stimulate our brains to think outside the box and generate innovative solutions. Imagine observing the way sunlight filters through leaves, inspiring you to design a new lighting system. This simple act of noticing can ignite your imagination and fuel a creative breakthrough.

1. Noticing the Sounds, Smells, and Textures of Inspiration beyond visuals

While sight plays a crucial role in the art of noticing, true creative inspiration often comes from engaging all our senses. The rhythmic tapping of rain on a window, the sweet fragrance of freshly baked bread, and the smooth texture of a worn stone – these sensory experiences can evoke emotions, memories, and associations that spark a creative fire.

Research by Dr. Charles Limb, a neuroscientist studying creativity, suggests that engaging multiple senses can activate different areas of the brain, leading to richer and more diverse creative thinking. Imagine smelling the salty air and hearing the crashing waves, inspiring you to write a poem about the ocean. This multi-sensory engagement can push you beyond the limitations of the visual and open doors to new realms of creativity.

2. Noticing beyond the Surface for Empathy and creativity

Creativity isn't just about generating ideas; it's about connecting with others and evoking emotions. By noticing the silent signs of human experience – a passing smile, a weary sigh, and a hesitant tone – we gain a deeper understanding of the human condition, fostering empathy and compassion. This, in turn, fuels our ability to create stories, art, and experiences that resonate with others on a deeper level.

Research by Dr. Lisa Feldman Barrett, a renowned neuroscientist, suggests that emotions are not simply internal feelings but also embodied experiences. By attuning ourselves to the emotions of others through mindful observation, we can tap into a shared wellspring of human experience, enriching our creative expression. Imagine observing the joy on a child's face at a playground, inspiring you to design a new toy that sparks imagination and laughter. This act of noticing not only fuels your creativity but also allows you to connect with others through a shared emotional experience.

3. Noticing as an Antidote for Burnout to Reclaim Your Creative Energy

Burnout, with its constant drain on our mental and emotional resources, can be a creativity killer. But the art of noticing offers a powerful antidote. By focusing on the present moment, appreciating the beauty around us, and connecting with others, we can fight the negativity and exhaustion that suppress our creative spark.

Research by Dr. Christina Maslach, a leading burnout researcher, highlights the importance of mindfulness and mind-body practices in reducing stress and burnout. By incorporating the art of noticing into our daily lives, we cultivate a sense of calm and presence, allowing our creative energy to replenish and flow more freely.

Putting Noticing Into Practice

By actively engaging with what we observe, we transform mere noticing into the fuel for creative expression. Here are some practical tips to unleash your creativity through noticing:

- **Carry a notebook:** Capture your observations – sights, sounds, smells, emotions – throughout the day. This acts as a repository of inspiration for later exploration.

- **Challenge your perspectives:** Look at familiar objects or situations from different angles. Ask yourself "What if?" and explore unconventional possibilities.

- **Create something every day:** Even a small sketch, a short poem, or a new recipe can keep your creative muscles active and open the door to bigger projects.

- **Collaborate with others:** Share your observations and brainstorm ideas together. Different perspectives can spark new insights and ignite collective creativity.

- **Embrace imperfection:** Don't be limited by perfectionism. The creative process is messy, playful, and full of experimentation.

As Jay Shetty reminds us, "The greatest discoveries often come from paying attention to the little things." Keep noticing, keep creating, and watch your creative potential blossom in ways you never imagined.

Kelvin's Experience

It will amuse you that I once taught a bunch of amazing kids one time in my life. Let me let you in on this experience...

I feel in love with teaching because it reminds me so much of my mum. In class, I was the life of the classroom, my energy used to bounce off the walls, infecting students with an contagious love for learning. But one day, my spark dimmed. Lesson plans felt like chores, jokes fell flat, and the twinkle in my eyes faded.

It wasn't the kids. They were still the same eager, curious bunch. It was me, stuck in a circle of routine and feeling the passion for teaching fade away like a sour meal. Grading papers felt like an endless sea, and lesson planning had become a stale sandwich I choked down every week.

One evening, while drowning my sorrows in a cup of lukewarm coffee, I stumbled on a flyer talking about a workshop on unleashing your creative potential and to my amazement – through noticing. It felt like a sign, a guiding light in the fog of my boredom. The next day, I found myself sitting in a room full of strangers, all seeking to rekindle their creative flames.

The workshop wasn't about fancy techniques or grand philosophies. It was about simple things, like paying attention to the way sunlight painted patterns on my classroom floor or listening to the souund of rustling leaves outside my window. They practiced noticing the good stuff, the tiny details that often get lost in the daily grind.

I said to myself, the art of noticing is a really broad subject. Just when you think you know it all, more keeps revealing itself. At first, it felt silly. Like playing childish games. But then, something shifted. I started noticing things about my students I'd never seen before. The shy girl's hidden talent for drawing, the quiet boy's love for birds, and the way their faces lit up when they understood a concept. My lessons, once routine, became opportunities to explore these discoveries. I incorporated their interests, creating a classroom that buzzed with curiosity and laughter.

The change wasn't just in the classroom. I started noticing the world around me, the bright colors of the market, the stories on the faces of strangers, the beauty in the ordinary, and even academically. The world, once ordinary, became a gold mine waiting to be explored.

My spark wasn't just rekindled, it exploded. My passion for teaching returned, but this time, it was richer, deeper, and fueled by the power of noticing. I wasn't just teaching history, I was igniting imaginations, opening doors to a world overflowing with wonder. And in doing so, I rediscovered the joy of learning, not just for my students, but for myself.

This is a warm reminder that sometimes, all it takes to reignite your passion is to simply **notice**. Pay attention to the world around you, the people in it, and the beauty that hides in the everyday. Because when you truly see, you not only rediscover the world, you rediscover yourself.

Part III: Mastering the Art of Noticing

This part isn't just about seeing things more clearly; it's about rekindling a lifelong love of discovery, reclaiming your attention from the digital void, and weaving the art of noticing into the very fabric of your life.

Chapter 7: Fueling Your Curiosity: Sparking a Lifelong Love of Discovery

"Old Man's Advice to Youth: 'Never Lose a Holy Curiosity.'" — **Albert Einstein**

Imagine a caterpillar, inching along a leaf. With every rustle, every glimmer of sunlight, every dewdrop, it still clings to a blade of grass. The caterpillar's tiny antennae twitch, picking up on the sound in the world around it. This, my friend, is the essence of curiosity – the insatiable hunger to know, explore, and unravel the mysteries that lie hidden in plain sight.

But what happens when the caterpillar transforms into a butterfly? Does the spark of curiosity fade, replaced by the appeal of flight? Sadly, for many of us, the answer is yes. We get caught up in our routines and the world shrinks to the size of our screens. But what if we could rekindle that childhood wonder, that unquenchable desire to explore the world around us?

The art of noticing as it concerns curiosity, is a way of seeing the world with fresh eyes, just by the simple act of truly noticing.

Why We Stop Asking Why

Today, we are bombarded with information, pushing us into a constant state of information consumption rather than active exploration. We scroll through headlines, watch pre-curated content, and rarely pause to truly question, wonder, and dig deeper. This passive engagement suffocates curiosity, leaving us feeling disconnected and uninspired.

Research by Dr. Celeste Kidd, a renowned cognitive scientist, suggests that curiosity plays a crucial role in cognitive development and learning. By asking questions and seeking answers, we engage our brains in active processing, strengthening neural pathways and fostering critical thinking skills. Imagine the difference between passively watching a nature documentary and actively researching the fascinating adaptations of a specific animal. The latter, fueled by curiosity, leads to deeper understanding and a more lasting impact on your knowledge base.

Noticing as the Gateway to Curiosity

The key to reigniting curiosity lies in nurturing the art of noticing. We have to actively engage our senses and awaken our minds to reach the extraordinary hidden inside the ordinary. Have you ever taken time to observe the delicate patterns on a peacock's wings? This simple act of noticing can spark curiosity about the peacock's life cycle and its role in the ecosystem.

How Noticing Fuels the Curiosity Flame

Noticing is an active process that engages multiple brain regions. Studies by Dr. Daniel Willingham, a cognitive scientist, suggest that novelty and surprise are key triggers for curiosity. When we notice something unexpected or unfamiliar, our brains release dopamine, a neurotransmitter associated with reward and motivation, pushing us to explore further and seek understanding.

Imagine noticing a strange bird you've never seen before. This unexpected observation triggers dopamine release, fueling your curiosity to identify the bird, learn about its habitat, and even share your discovery with others. This cycle of noticing, surprise, and exploration keeps the flame of curiosity burning bright.

Expanding the Sensory Playground of Curiosity

The world is a multi-sensory experience, and each sense can be a gateway to igniting curiosity.

Research by Dr. Paul Ekman, a renowned psychologist, highlights the power of emotional engagement in fostering curiosity. When we connect with something on an emotional level, our motivation to understand it deepens. Imagine the awe you feel gazing at a starry night sky, especially if you are doing this with someone you care deeply for. This emotional connection fuels your curiosity about the universe, its mysteries, and its vastness. By engaging all our senses and connecting emotionally with the world around us, we expand the playground of curiosity and open doors to endless discovery.

Cultivating a Lifelong Love of Discovery: Practical Tips

By nurturing your newfound curiosity, you embark on a lifelong journey of discovery. Here are some practical tips to keep the flame burning:

1. **Embrace the Beginner's Mind:**

   - **Challenge Assumptions:** Question the familiar. Don't accept things at face value. Ask "why" and "how" more often, even about seemingly mundane things.

   - **Step outside Your Comfort Zone:** Try new things, visit unfamiliar places, and engage with people from different backgrounds. Embrace the awkwardness and discomfort of learning something new.

   - **Read Children's Books:** Rekindle the wonder of exploration by revisiting stories written for curious young minds. They often ask thought-provoking questions and present fresh perspectives.

2. **Engage Your Senses:**

   - **Become a Sensory Detective:** Pay close attention to the sights, sounds, smells, tastes, and textures around you. Notice each detail, the unexpected changes, and the unique qualities of each experience.

- **Expand Your Sensory Palette:** Explore new sensory experiences. Try exotic foods, listen to unfamiliar music, or visit museums with interactive exhibits. Engage with the world in ways you haven't before.

- **Practice Mindful Observation:** Take walks or spend time in nature to be present and fully experience your surroundings. Focus on the details, the sensations, and the emotions evoked by the environment.

3. **Question and Investigate:**

- **Follow Your "Why's":** Don't let your curiosity fade after the initial spark. Research the answers to your questions, delve deeper into the topic, and connect with experts or communities of like-minded individuals.

- **Become an Amateur Scientist:** Conduct small experiments in your everyday life. Observe, hypothesize, test, and draw conclusions. Cultivate a playful spirit of inquiry and experimentation.

- **Turn Everyday Experiences into Mysteries:** Look for puzzles and questions within your daily routines. Analyze problems, explore different perspectives, and find creative solutions.

4. **Connect and Share:**

- **Share Your Discoveries:** Discuss your curiosities with friends, family, or online communities. Explain your findings, ask for their perspectives, and learn from their experiences.

- **Become a Curious Collaborator:** Partner with others on projects that ignite your curiosity. Learn from their expertise, share your knowledge, and co-create discoveries.

- **Teach What You Learn:** Share your knowledge and enthusiasm with others. Mentor younger generations, give talks, or write articles to inspire others on their journeys of curiosity.

5. **Celebrate the Journey:**

- **Find Joy in the Process:** Don't get discouraged if you don't have all the answers. Enjoy the process of asking questions, exploring possibilities, and learning something new every day.

- **Embrace the Unexpected:** Remember, curiosity can lead you down unexpected paths and open doors to unforeseen discoveries. Be open to the surprises and detours along the way.

- **Reward Yourself for Being Curious:** Acknowledge your efforts to cultivate curiosity. Celebrate your progress, no matter how small, and fuel your motivation to keep exploring and discovering.

By incorporating these practical steps into your daily life, you can transform from a passive observer into an active explorer, igniting a flame of wonder that will guide you on a path of continuous learning, growth, and joy.

Oliver's Experience

Meet Oliver, a man whose enthusiasm for the past rivaled Indiana Jones and was starting to feel like an old forgotten bicycle abandoned in the basement. Once, he found joy in every archeological escapade he embarked on, but now, sifting through ancient pottery ruins felt more like sorting laundry – unexciting and dull.

It wasn't that the digs weren't interesting anymore. The abandoned temple in Guatemala was swarming with secrets, each unearthed brick wanting to tell its forgotten tales. But the spark in Oliver's eyes, the one that ignited with every discovery had dimmed. Now he was indifferent.

He'd blame it on fatigue, the relentless sun beating down on his already weary shoulders. Or maybe it was the grant rejections, the constant struggle to secure funding for his passion project. But deep down, Oliver knew it was more than that. The flame of curiosity, the very fuel that propelled him through years of research and countless excavations, was flickering dangerously low.

One evening Oliver slumped over a pile of dusty journals and a quote caught his attention: "Fuel Your Curiosity through Noticing." It was like a jolt of electricity. Noticing? Wasn't that what he did for a living – noticing the tiniest details, the hidden patterns that spoke of lives long gone?

But what if he applied that same noticing to his own life? Instead of focusing on the labor of paperwork, could he find wonder in the sunrise painting the temple walls, or the laughter of children playing amidst the ruins? The next day, Oliver embarked on a silent experiment. He put away his magnifying glass and simply observed. He watched the fireflies dance against the evening sky, listened to the sweet rhythm of raindrops on his tent, and marveled at the resilience of a tiny wildflower pushing through cracked pavement.

The world, once boring, came alive in a series of sights and sounds. The ordinary transformed into adventures. The grumpy cook's whistle became a secret code, the worn-out map in his pocket, a portal to countless stories.

Slowly, the spark in Oliver's eyes reignited. His notes came alive with newfound enthusiasm, his lectures bursting with the infectious energy of rediscovered passion. He started a blog, sharing his adventures in noticing and inspiring others to find magic in the everyday.

Oliver's journey is a quiet reminder that curiosity isn't a finite resource; it is a muscle that needs to be exercised by the simple act of noticing the extraordinary in the ordinary. And in that noticing, he found not just his passion, but a renewed appreciation for the world, and his place in its fascinating story.

Chapter 8: Taming the Digital Deluge: Neuroscience-Based Strategies for Reclaiming Your Attention and Living Healthier Lives

"Technology is a useful servant but a dangerous master." -
Alfred North Whitehead

Remember the days when you could lose yourself in a book for hours, or savor a conversation without a constant buzz interrupting your thoughts? In our digital age, the relentless barrage of notifications, social media updates, and endless content streams has become a constant assault on our attention. Jay Shetty emphasizes that we are not designed for this constant stimulation and the consequences are far-reaching. Here, we are looking at neuroscience-based strategies to tame the digital surge and reclaim our focus and health through the power of noticing.

The Digital Age's Toll on Our Minds

The human brain is wired for innovation and reward, making it highly prone to the dopamine-fueled loops of digital distractions. With every notification, every like, and every click, our brains release a small burst of pleasure, urging us to seek more. This constant stimulation, however, comes at a cost. Research by Dr. Adam Gazzaley, a renowned neuroscientist, highlights the negative impact of digital distractions on cognitive function, attention span, and even empathy. Imagine trying to write a report while your phone buzzes with notifications; the mental juggling act disrupts your focus, hinders your ability to process information, and ultimately, affects the quality of your work.

The Neuroscience of Attention Fatigue

The constant switching between tasks and information sources not only fragments our attention but also depletes our cognitive resources. This mental fatigue, known as attention fatigue, can manifest as difficulty concentrating, increased irritability, and even emotional dysregulation. Research by Dr. Christine Neupert, a cognitive psychologist, suggests that this fatigue isn't simply a matter of willpower; it's a neurological phenomenon caused by the brain's inability to sustain constant attention switching. Imagine feeling overwhelmed after a day of scrolling through social media or checking emails. This isn't just laziness; it's your brain crying out for a break from the digital overload.

Reclaiming Your Attention through Noticing

Amid the digital flood, the answer lies not in fighting technology, but in reclaiming your attention through the power of noticing. Jay Shetty advises us to quiet the mind and tune into the present moment. By cultivating mindful awareness of your internal and external environment, you can break free from the automatic pull of distractions and regain control over your focus.

Neuroscience-Based Strategies for Noticing

Attention:

- **Mindfulness practice:** Train your attention to focus on the present moment and be aware of how you interact with technology. Meditation apps like Ten Percent Happier, Headspace, Buddhify, Calm, or Insight Timer can be helpful for beginners.

- **Identify attention traps:** Notice what triggers you to mindlessly scroll or check your phone. Are there certain apps, notifications, or social media platforms?

- **Minimize distractions:** Turn off notifications, silence your phone, and close unnecessary browser tabs. Consider using apps that block distracting websites or set time limits for social media use.

Intention:

- **Set clear goals:** Before going online, ask yourself what you want to achieve. Are you checking for important updates, researching a topic, or connecting with friends?

- **Single-tasking:** Focus on one task at a time instead of multitasking. This helps your brain process information more efficiently and reduces the feeling of overwhelm.

- **Timeboxing:** Set a timer for how long you will spend online and stick to it. This can help prevent you from getting lost in the digital world.

Awareness:

- **Track your tech use:** There are apps available that can track how much time you spend on different apps and websites such as *Usage Time*. This awareness can help you identify areas where you can cut back.

- **Notice your emotional state:** Pay attention to how you feel before, during, and after using technology. Are you feeling stressed, anxious, or unproductive? If so, take a break and do something relaxing.

- **Reward yourself:** When you successfully stick to your goals, reward yourself with something you enjoy. This will help you stay motivated and on track.

- **Keep your phone out of sight:** Put your phone away in a drawer or another room when you're not using it. This will help reduce the temptation to check it constantly.

- **Create tech-free zones:** Designate certain areas of your home or office as tech-free zones, such as the bedroom or dinner table.

- **Connect with others:** Spend time with friends and family in person or over video chat. This can help you feel more connected and reduce your reliance on technology.

- **Seek professional help:** If you're struggling to manage your digital habits, consider talking to a therapist or counselor who specializes in technology addiction.

Building a healthier digital life through noticing

Every day, you wake up, instinctively reach for your phone, and get sucked into a vortex of news, social media, and notifications. Hours melt away before you realize it, leaving you feeling drained, distracted, and disconnected from your own life. This, unfortunately, is the reality for many of us in today's digital overflow.

The good news is there is a way to regain your attention, your health, and your life, not by abandoning technology, but by harnessing the power of noticing.

The More We Scroll, the Less We Live

Ironically, the very tools designed to connect us are isolating us from the present moment, which is crucial for our health and well-being. Dr. Barbara Fredrickson, a renowned positivity researcher, emphasizes the importance of present-moment awareness for stress reduction and emotional well-being. Yet, our digital habits pull us away from the present, fostering a disconnect from the sights, sounds, and textures of our immediate environment. Imagine mindlessly scrolling through social media instead of savoring a delicious meal or appreciating the beauty of nature. This digital distraction robs us of the present-moment experiences that nourish our minds and bodies, contributing to feelings of isolation and dissatisfaction.

Building Resilient Habits: Practical Steps for Everyday Life

Now, let's translate awareness into action with these practical strategies:

1. **Reclaim Your Mornings:**

   - **Start with intention:** Before picking up your phone, set an intention for your morning. Will it be focused on work, mindful movement, or simply enjoying a cup of coffee?

   - **Embrace a "tech-free buffer zone":** Designate the first 30-60 minutes of your day as tech-free. Use this time for activities that ground you and set the tone for a mindful day.

   - **Utilize technology consciously:** If you need to use technology for work or communication, set specific goals and time limits. Avoid multitasking and be present in the task at hand.

2. Tame Notifications:

- **Identify the culprits:** Analyze which apps and notifications are the biggest distractions. Turn off unnecessary alerts and consider silencing all notifications during focused work periods.

- **Embrace batch checking:** Instead of constantly checking your phone, designate specific times to check emails and social media. This reduces the disruptive "ping-pong" effect of notifications.

- **Utilize "Do Not Disturb" and airplane mode:** Don't be afraid to disconnect completely when needed. Use these features to create tech-free zones throughout your day, allowing for deep work, relaxation, and quality time with loved ones.

3. Cultivate Mindful Tech Use:

- **Engage with intention:** Before opening an app, ask yourself, "What value will this add to my life right now?" Be mindful of the content you consume and avoid mindless scrolling.

- **Set time limits:** Utilize features like app timers to limit your screen time on specific platforms. This helps prevent getting sucked into endless scrolling and reclaim control over your time.

- **Connect with purpose:** Use technology for meaningful interactions and creative expression. Join online communities, learn new skills, or connect with loved ones through video calls.

4. Prioritize Sleep Hygiene:

- **Avoid screens before bed:** The blue light emitted from screens disrupts sleep patterns. Put away your phone at least an hour before bedtime and create a relaxing bedtime routine.

- **Embrace mindfulness practices:** Utilize meditation or deep breathing exercises before bed to calm your mind and prepare for sleep.

- **Create a sleep-conducive environment:** Ensure your bedroom is dark, quiet, and cool for optimal sleep quality.

5. Nurture Your Body and Mind:

- **Move your body:** Regular physical activity is crucial for physical and mental health. Engage in activities you enjoy, whether it's walking, dancing, or playing a sport.

- **Connect with nature:** Spend time outdoors, immersing yourself in nature. This reduces stress, improves mood, and fosters a sense of well-being.

- **Practice mindfulness:** Incorporate mindfulness practices like meditation or yoga into your daily routine to cultivate present-moment awareness and manage stress effectively.

As we conclude this chapter, ask yourself these questions;

- When do I reach for my phone? Am I bored, seeking validation, or avoiding discomfort?

- How does using technology make me feel? Do I feel energized, connected, or anxious and drained?

- Does my technology use align with my values and goals?

These questions illuminate the unconscious patterns driving your digital habits. As you go on to build resilient digital habits with the help of noticing, be aware that there will be setbacks, but be kind to yourself, celebrate your progress, and keep coming back to the power of noticing. With consistent effort and mindful practice, you can reclaim control over your digital life, cultivate healthier habits, and live a more fulfilling life.

Kelvin's Experience

Today I also own a laundry mart asides being a doctor. Man, let me tell you, I once drowned. Not in water, but in information. Emails, news blasts, industry reports – they all buzzed around me like digital mosquitoes, demanding my attention. At first, I juggled them like a pro, feeling on top of my game. But later, that juggling act became a desperate scramble. Orders got messed up, meetings slipped through the cracks, and I honestly felt like a sleep-deprived hamster hopped up on five espressos.

My brain, once as sharp as a freshly pressed shirt, turned foggy. Decisions became muddled, and my small laundry business, built on crisp whites and fluffy towels, resembled a tangled mess of mismatched socks and forgotten dry cleaning. Even Linda, my saint of an assistant, started giving me concerned looks. It was clear: something had to give.

Then, one night I decided to revisit my learnings on the art of noticing and stumbled upon an chapter that spoke of : "Taming the Digital barrag" Intrigued, I clicked, and a whole new world opened up. It talked about "attention residue," the mental clutter left behind by information overload, and how it messes with your focus and decision-making. It also mentioned "noticing," this simple yet powerful practice of just paying attention to the present moment, without judgment.

Now, at first, I scoffed. Noticing? What did that have to do with laundry and spreadsheets? But the more I read, the more it resonated. So, I started small. Five minutes each morning, just observing my surroundings: watching the beautiful sunrise, the warmth of my cat's fur as it glides on my skin tenderly, the rich taste of my coffee, and the birds that take turns to come chirping at my windowsill that I have ignored for quite some time. Nothing earth-shattering, but a start.

Gradually, noticing became more deliberate. Before checking emails, I'd take a mindful breath, resisting the urge to multitask like a maniac. During Linda's reports, I'd truly listen, focusing on her concerns instead of planning my next move in my head. Slowly, the fog started to lift.

The joy of focusing on one thing at a time returned. Decisions became clearer, and meetings more productive. Even Linda seemed lighter, her worried glances replaced by genuine smiles. The business, once on the brink of chaos, regained its rhythm.

Now, don't get me wrong, the digital deluge still tries to pull me under sometimes. But now, I have a lifeguard: the power of noticing. I learned that amidst the information storm, there's an oasis of calm waiting to be discovered. And in that calm, I found not just a better CEO, but a clearer, more present human being. And that, my friends, is the most valuable laundry I could ever clean.

Chapter 9

Living a noticing life free of stress and full of Positive Thinking

"You cannot control the waves, but you can learn to surf." -
Jon Kabat-Zinn

Are you the one to wake up, greet the sunrise with a genuine smile, and savor the day's possibilities? Do you wake up stressed? Or does it bounce off you like a feather on a hurricane? Think about this for a minute.

It's best to wake up with a positive perspective radiating from within like sunshine. This isn't a fairy tale; it is mindful living after mastering the art of noticing and this can be your narrative.

The key to unlocking inner peace and silencing stress lies in cultivating mindfulness. Think of it like hitting the pause button on your mental overdrive. From Jay Shetty's teaching, we've learned that "awareness is the first step to change," and noticing empowers you to become aware of your thoughts, emotions, and surroundings. This awareness gives you the power to choose how you respond to life's inevitable curveballs.

30-Day Noticing Toolkit

You can ignite your journey towards a more mindful, stress-free, and positive life through the following:

Day 1-10: plant the Seed of Awareness		
Day	Practice	Purpose
1-5	**The Mindful Minute:** Set a daily reminder to pause, breathe, and observe your surroundings for 60 seconds. No judgment, just notice.	**Tune into the present moment and awaken your senses.**
6-10	**Sensory Adventures:** Engage your senses throughout your day. Savor the texture of your clothes, listen to the birdsong, or smell the coffee brewing.	**Break autopilot and appreciate the richness of everyday experiences.**
8-10	**Gratitude Noticing:** Before bed, reflect on three things you're grateful for that day. Write them down or share them with someone you love.	**Shift your focus to the positive and cultivate an attitude of appreciation.**

Day 11-20: Cultivate the Art of Observation

Day	Practice	Purpose
11-15	**Noticing Walks:** Walk mindfully, focusing on the details: textures underfoot, shapes of clouds, and patterns in nature. Capture observations in photos or notes.	**Engage your senses and discover the hidden beauty in your surroundings.**
16-20	**Noticing Interactions:** During conversations, truly listen, observe nonverbal cues, and ask thoughtful questions. Notice your own reactions and emotions.	**Connect more deeply with others and gain insights into yourself and others.**

Day 21-30: Transform Your Life Through Noticing

Day	Practice	Purpose
21-25	**Activity Noticing:** Choose an activity you often do on	**Increase self-awareness and identify**

	autopilot (eating, commuting, and working). Observe your thoughts, emotions, and sensations with curiosity. Ask: "What can I learn from this experience?"	**opportunities for change.**
26-30	**Challenge Negative Thoughts:** When negativity arises, notice it without judgment. Ask: "Is this thought helpful? Is it true?" Replace it with a more positive and realistic one.	**Cultivate a positive mindset and break free from limiting beliefs.**

Recall that while noticing fosters joy and positivity, it's not about ignoring life's challenges. It's about acknowledging them with mindfulness and acceptance as we learned about the 4 four honorable truths to note by Buddha. Notice difficult emotions without judgment, and use them as opportunities for growth and learning. Remember, even negativity holds valuable lessons. By noticing it with awareness, you can navigate it with resilience and emerge stronger.

When you notice a wave of sadness: Observe it without resistance. Ask yourself: "What is this sadness trying to tell me?" Perhaps it's a signal to prioritize self-care, reach out for support, or simply acknowledge a loss. By noticing and accepting these emotions, you open the door to healing and personal growth.

Lastly, your noticing toolkit isn't a rigid script; it's an evolving venture. Explore different noticing practices, experiment with what resonates with you, and most importantly, keep growing.

EXERCISES ON THE ART OF NOTICING

Below are the "Art of Noticing" exercises I promised at the beginning of the book. These exercises aren't just for fun, it's a way to fine-tune your brain to notice more of the world. The more you practice, the more you see. And who knows? The art of noticing might just reveal a hidden layer of the world around you.

Fun Exercise 2

Take a look at this intriguing scene bustling with action. Look closer at the image and pick just 10 things you can see. Go on, take your time and observe...

Ready? Here are some items you might have listed:

1. A large armored vehicle.

2. Police van.

3. Riot police with a shield.

4. A couple of palm trees.

5. A protester with a gun.

6. Barricades.

7. A fallen person.

8. A megaphone.

9. Street signs.

10. An assortment of objects on the ground – could be rocks or perhaps tear gas canisters.

But here's where it gets really interesting. What did you miss?

The Art of Noticing is about seeing more than the most immediate or obvious elements. It's about attention to detail. So, let's see what you might have overlooked:

- The shadows cast by the trees and people, offering an indication of the time of day.

- The five bags of money; two of them are open while the other three are closed.

- The direction the police are facing, which might tell us where the main action is happening.

- The pattern of the barricades, which appear to be strategically placed.

- The police man pointing a gun behind the criminals and they are unaware.

- The police man at the other side of the road observing as the event unfolds with a baton in hand.

- The specific stance of the criminals, is it aggressive or peaceful?
- The number of policemen carrying a long and short gun.

Did you catch all of that? If not, don't sweat it.

If you didn't, what must have occurred is Change Blindness. Change blindness is a surprising perceptual phenomenon that occurs when a change in a visual stimulus is introduced and the observer does not notice it. For instance, imagine you're looking at a picture of a street scene, and when the image is briefly interrupted, an object in the scene changes color or disappears entirely. Often, people fail to notice the change.

Researchers Rensink, O'Regan, and Clark (1997) demonstrated this effect in a study where they asked participants to detect changes in photographic images that were flicked back and forth with a blank grey image in between. Even when changes were significant, such as the disappearance of an engine on an aircraft, participants often failed to notice them immediately. This happens because visual attention is a prerequisite for perceiving change; unless a particular element within the visual field captures our attention, we're likely to miss a change.

The implications of change blindness are profound in everyday life. It means that our perception of the world is not as stable and continuous as we might assume. Our visual system constructs a representation of the world from moment to moment, often filling in gaps with our expectations and prior knowledge.

Noticing is not just about a one-time observation but requires continuous monitoring and updating of the visual scene. To notice changes or to pick up on subtle details, we must learn to periodically shift our attention and not assume that once we've seen a scene, we know all there is to know about it.

In your day-to-day life, when you practice noticing more of your environment, you are combating inattentional blindness. This can lead to a fuller appreciation of our world, help us recognize opportunities and dangers we might otherwise miss, and enrich our experiences in every moment. So, take a second look—what else can you notice now?

Here's another interesting image, take a critical look at the image above and write down the 10 things you can notice from it. Don't rush, really soak it in.

Okay, what did you spot? Maybe you saw:

1. A pedestrian crossing sign.

2. A person walking a dog.

3. A cyclist.

4. A white car.

5. The building looks modern.

6. The cyclist wearing a hat.

7. The building has multiple windows.

8. A street with a crosswalk.

9. People wearing backpacks.

10. Some sort of boxes on the sidewalk.

But wait, there's more to this picture. Let's peel back another layer and see what you might have missed – the delicate details that require you to master "The Art of Noticing":

- Just two people are wearing white footwear.

- The woman who is about to use the zebra crossing is on the phone.

- The stars around the lady with a cup of coffee indicates how hyper and positive she is feeling.

- The dog has a white collar.

- The slight open door of the building – what's happening inside?

- The cyclist is just about to take off because he has his left foot on the ground?

- The windows of the white car is tinted, we can't see through.

- The lady walking towards the cyclist has a bag with two black locks.

Did you catch all these details? If some of them slipped past you, it's completely natural. Cognitive neuroscience is the idea of "neural adaptation" or "sensory adaptation." This is the process by which our neurons decrease their activity in response to a constant stimulus. Our brains are designed to respond to change and novelty; when the same stimulus is presented for a long time, we actually become less sensitive to it. This is why, if you're in a room with a constant hum from an air conditioner, after a while, you may not notice the sound at all.

This principle applies to vision as well. When we look at a scene, we initially notice the new or changing elements, but as those elements become familiar, they fade into the background of our conscious perception. This phenomenon can be explained by the theory of predictive coding, which suggests that the brain is constantly generating and updating a model of the environment based on incoming sensory information and prior expectations (Rao and Ballard, 1999). When something doesn't change or doesn't match our predictive model, it becomes less salient and we are less likely to consciously notice it.

Now, apply this to the exercise with the image. When you first look at the scene, your brain is identifying changes and creating a model of what's happening. As you continue to look, the static elements become 'predicted' by your brain and are effectively tuned out. You're less likely to notice them unless you make a conscious effort to refresh your perception and challenge your brain's model by looking for things that you haven't already labeled and understood.

This is where the "Art of Noticing" comes into play. It's about consciously refreshing your perception, looking for the unexpected, and not allowing your brain to become too comfortable with the initial model it has created. By doing so, you can counteract neural adaptation and maintain a high level of sensitivity to your environment.

By understanding the science behind noticing, we can better train ourselves to be observant, to refresh our gaze frequently, and to engage more deeply with the world around us. It's not just about seeing; it's about actively perceiving and being present in the moment. This can enhance our experiences, make us more mindful, and even improve our memory of events because we're paying better attention to the details. So, as you look back at the image, challenge your brain: What are the details that have become invisible due to neural adaptation, and how can you bring them back into view?

Check out this image packed with all sorts of curious details. It's a bit like a detective's puzzle, isn't it? I want you to play detective now. Scan the scene and spot 10 items. Observe like Sherlock would and jot them down when you're ready.

Okay, have your list? Let's compare notes! You probably picked out some of these:

1. A detective smoking pipe.
2. A police officer's cap.
3. A pair of handcuffs.
4. A magnifying glass.
5. A fingerprint.
6. Blood splatters.
7. A scale of justice.
8. Bags of money with dollar signs.
9. Two guns.
10. Brown leather gloves.

Now, let's sharpen our noticing skills. What might you have skimmed over?

- The frame of a man in checked pattern merging him with the background.
- The compass close to the detective.
- Pocket knife in-between the guns.
- The man in black holding a knife.
- The stack of dollar bill.
- The different shapes of red in the blood splatter, indicating perhaps the manner the victim was harmed.
- The slight shadow under the money, giving it depth.
- The bullet standing alone close to the police officer's cap.
- The detective is wearing an inner grey shirt.
- The dollar signs on the bags of money are reversed/placed wrongly.

Why are these things easy to miss? It's due to a fascinating aspect of our cognitive abilities: the spotlight theory of attention. This theory suggests that our attention works somewhat like a spotlight. Just as a spotlight illuminates only a small area of a stage, our cognitive spotlight controls the information we become conscious of and can process in detail. This means that our attention is limited and can only be focused on a small portion of our sensory environment at a time (Posner et al., 1980).

When we looked at the detective-themed image, you were asked to focus your spotlight on certain items. Naturally, this limited focus can cause us to miss other details, no matter how obvious they might be upon a second glance.

Furthermore, there's another layer to our attention: the distinction between "top-down" and "bottom-up" processes. "Top-down" attention is driven by your intentions and what you decide to focus on; it's like when you're looking for clues in the image because you're playing detective. "Bottom-up" attention, on the other hand, is driven by stimuli that stand out due to their properties, like bright colors or a loud noise, which might explain why the blood splatters are immediately noticeable (Theeuwes, 2010).

Combining these two processes, we start to understand why certain items in the image, especially those that are less salient or do not align with our immediate objectives, can escape our notice.

This is why "The Art of Noticing" isn't just about looking harder, but about looking smarter—about training your cognitive spotlight to move around and catch details that aren't immediately drawn into focus by either top-down or bottom-up processes. It's about being curious and intentionally widening your beam to take in more of your surroundings.

By understanding and practicing this, you can improve your ability to notice the richness of detail that the world offers, whether it's in an image, a busy street, or a conversation with a friend. So, let's look again. Move your spotlight. What else is there in the image that you didn't see before?

Take a good look at the above image. It's more than just a pretty picture, it's a challenge for your eyes and mind. Can you spot 5 things in this image? Give it a shot before reading on. Jot them down somewhere. Go on, take your time and observe...

Done? Okay, let's see how you did. You probably noticed the obvious stuff:

1. The mountain range
2. The pine trees
3. The cabins
4. The clouds

5. The winding path

But did you catch these less obvious details? These are the things that might slip by if you're not practicing the art of noticing:

6. The texture of the wooden cabin walls - see those lines? That's the wood grain.

7. The smoke coming from one of the cabins - someone's probably cozy by a fire in there.

8. The different strokes that show direction of the wind - look at how the trees bend slightly to one side.

9. The shadows under the roof eaves - they tell us where the light is coming from.

10. The footsteps on the path - a sign of life, someone's been here not too long ago.

But why do we miss these things? Science tells us that our brains are wired to sieve out information deemed unnecessary. According to a study from Harvard University, people can suffer from 'inattentional blindness,' where we are so focused on one task that we completely miss other obvious, but unexpected things (like the famous 'invisible gorilla' experiment).

Moreover, the human brain is not a passive recipient of information. According to research published in Nature Reviews Neuroscience, it is an active data seeker, always predicting and interpreting what we see based on past experiences. So, if you haven't trained your brain to look for the less obvious, it'll stick to the basics.

So, what did you see? Was there anything I missed? Write it down. After all, noticing is a personal art, and your canvas might look different from mine.

Conclusion

Congratulation!!! You've read the book up to this point. Don't put down the knowledge you've acquired as you get ready to dive into the "now."

But tell me, how does it feel? Perhaps familiar, perhaps a little different? If you've been paying attention, and cultivating the art of noticing, you'll know not to notice with judgment, but with more compassion, less reactivity, and more keenly.

The art of noticing unlocks a "being" mode in our brains, one that thrives on present-moment awareness. In contrast to the "doing" mode, driven by stories and plans, this is an experiential state where the insula (bodily sensations) and anterior cingulate cortex (attention) light up and meditators have more control over switching between these modes, choosing how to engage with the world.

Mindfulness is a simple, accessible superpower. No expensive tools, no agenda, just pure attention, presence, and decision-making based on innate wisdom unearthed through practice. Whether it's physical or mental challenges, relationship woes, or existential worry, meeting them mindfully helps.

As we deepen our practice, we will see how pleasure cravings lead to pain, and resistance to suffering amplifies it. We will break free from childhood conditioning and societal pressures, choosing actions that bring genuine contentment. We will spend less time in our heads, realizing busy minds don't solve busy-mind problems. We will find more ease, less reactivity, and a deeper appreciation for the world's beauty, without getting attached. We will learn to ride the inevitable ups and downs, transforming life's insults into joys.

As you go on, know that there are no guarantees. This path can be challenging, filled with unexpected twists and turns. We might encounter physical pain, strong emotions, and uncomfortable truths. The truth is transformation rarely looks like what we expect it to look like. With time inner peace and even joy will be evident.

Ultimately, the art of noticing connects us with our world, frees us from stress, allows us to think more positively, and manifests more fully and compassionately in the world. This is one of the greatest gifts we can offer to ourselves and everyone around us.